Dear African American Girl,

Life Lessons of an African Girl in an American World

Amarachi Akwarandu, M.S.

Dear African American Girl,
Life Lessons of an African Girl in an American World

Copyright © 2021 Amarachi Akwarandu

ISBN-13: 9798599829867

Cover Design by Miryam Copara-Ojeda | Instagram @darkstar.creations

This book is dedicated to all of the African American girls and young women trying to understand their identity and place in the world. You are not meant to fit in or be ordinary. You are <u>extra</u>ordinary.

Contents

Chapter 1:

"Do you have a nickname?"

I've always dreaded the first day of school, especially when it was time for the teacher to take attendance. My name was always the first name called on the attendance sheet and each time, teachers BUTCHERED it. I mean, not only did they mispronounce my name, but they also pronounced letters and sounds that weren't even there! How in the world do you get "Mariachi band", "A-mark-key", "Mer-reach-ee", or "Anarchy", from the name "Amarachi"? And every time a teacher or someone else had trouble pronouncing my name, they always asked the same exact question, *"do you have a nickname?"*

Now, many students in middle school and high school would've responded with "sure, you can call me [blank]." And some would even allow their teacher to create a nickname for them to quickly end the embarrassment of having their name mispronounced, but NOT ME! Even when the rest of the class laughed at the mispronunciation of my name, my response to having a nickname has always been *"no."* And I'd correct them until they could properly pronounce my name, no matter how long it took because just like the popular phrase coined by the comedian Kevin Hart, "You gon' learn today!"

You're probably wondering, "why on earth would you make things harder for yourself and not go by an easier or more "ordinary" nickname?" Well, the answer is simple. I am not meant to be ordinary and neither is my name. I also believe that the same way people can learn to pronounce the names "Ashley", "Nicole", and even "Arnold Schwazenegger", is the same way they can learn to pronounce my name. Every single name, regardless of how short, long, or complex, has to be learned. Think about it, no one comes into this world knowing how to pronounce names or words. As babies and young children, we learn how to say things through what we hear and practice. The only reason we know anything, right or wrong, is because we are taught. And with anything new we are trying to learn, with some effort, repetition, and time, we will learn them.

So, the problem isn't being able to pronounce a name because clearly anything can be learned. The real problem is whether people are willing to learn your name and the fact that some people even feel inconvenienced by a name they have never seen before. But guess what? It really does not matter what's easy or convenient for other people to pronounce! WE were inconvenienced when you mispronounced our name! WE were inconvenienced when the class laughed at us! WE were inconvenienced when you wanted us to think of a nickname for you to call us! WE were inconvenienced when you called us something other than our real name!

By now, you're probably thinking, well what if my close friends and family call me a cute nickname or pet name? I'm definitely not saying there is anything wrong with being called a pet name like princess, sweetheart, love, and so on by people you're close to. But what I do want you understand is that there is a difference between being called a pet name/nickname by people who know and love you versus having your name shortened or changed by people who don't. The key difference is the meaning behind the name. One expresses love and nurture, while the other expresses discomfort and a degree of intolerance. One is a form acceptance, while the other is a form of rejection. One draws you closer, while the other pushes you away. One is made with purpose and sentiment, while the other is just made out of convenience. If you do not take anything else away from this book, I want you to understand this:

Life Lesson 1: You should never allow anyone to change your name for their own convenience.

Regardless of what your name is, never allow someone to change it to something easier or more "ordinary" for them because you are not ordinary and neither is your name. Your name means something. Your name is powerful. Your name IS power. I personally believe that your name has an influence on who you are and how your life plays out. For example, my name is Amarachi and it means *Grace of God*. Now some people with the same name, may just go by "Chi", which means "God" or "Amara", which just means *grace*. But neither names alone mean the same thing together. Anyone can have or be shown grace, but the grace of God is a grace like none other and is the most powerful of all.

I believe that what you allow people to call you, is what you begin to answer to, believe, and manifest within your life. I don't know about you, but I refuse to be or have a life that reflects someone else's convenience or their own perception about me. By now you're probably wondering how in the world a simple nickname can influence your entire life. Well it's simple. When you allow people to call you something, after a while, you start to believe it. And when you start to believe it, whether you know it or not, you view and interpret events in your life through that lens, further reinforcing that belief. Then, when you start to see things through that lens, you notice and even attract more and more things that supports this belief into your life. It literally boils down to one of the most basic yet powerful universal laws – *The Law of Attraction* - "like attracts like." So, when you believe something, you attract things that align with that belief.

Here's another example. Let's say your family nicknamed you "*Speed*" because as a toddler, you were always moving and getting into things so fast. And as you got older, the nickname stuck with you and you often sped through schoolwork and sports, which might have been a good thing depending on how you look at it. But this speed also transferred into other areas of your life like speeding too fast into friendships and romantic relationships, completely missing the red flags telling you that these people might be toxic.

You also sped too fast into careers and found yourself often switching because you didn't take enough time to make these choices and weren't able to recognize that the career wasn't for you until sometime after you had already started. At some point, these speedy decisions and consequences that cause you to constantly start, stop, and then restart over and over again, builds up and can lead you feel mentally exhausted and burned out. The thing about speeding is that you will always run out of gas much quicker. And even though you may be able to get to your destination faster, at some point you will find yourself stuck or forced to come to a complete stop.

Okay, I know for some of you that might have been kind of an extreme example, but the take home message is this: when you allow people to call you something outside of your name, you're no longer being called to be who you were meant to be. I believe that I am the walking definition of the grace of God and everything that has happened in my life from birth to now, literally reflects that. During labor and delivery, my mother first gave birth to my twin sister naturally. And as with twins, my arrival was expected moments later, but unfortunately that was not the case. Seconds turned into minutes and minutes turned into hours, yet I was still unable to leave my mother's womb. You can imagine the stress and concern my parents were under, wondering what was going on with their other daughter and why was she not responsive.

Normally under these situations, it's easy to assume that I was gone or at least very close to it. What made the situation more difficult was that the doctors refused to take my mother's request for a c-section seriously, despite knowing my mother was a registered nurse and midwife. Unfortunately, many black women's experience and needs in America are not taken seriously by their doctors especially during childbirth. But sometime later, my mother was rushed into the operating room for a c-section, and almost three hours later and by the grace of God, I was born.

Now, I'm sure there are some critics saying, "it's not that serious, it's just a name". But it's not just a name, it's YOUR name and it belongs to you. It is what you answer to and what helps tell your story. Dear

African American girl, your story is powerful. If you allow people to take away something as simple as your name, imagine what else they'll take. Better yet, what else will you be willing to give up?

Life Lesson 2: Never allow anyone to diminish or take your power away!

Throughout this book, I will be asking you a number of questions to get you thinking and posing one challenge after each chapter. For some of you, you might not be able to answer these questions at first and for some of you, your answers may change by the time you finish this book or sometime after. But you know what? It's all completely okay. The goal is to help you start thinking about who you are, the things you've experienced, and who you would like to be.

1. What is your name?

2. What does your name mean?

   -What does the meaning of your name mean to you?

3. If your name has no literal meaning or translates to an inanimate object or day, or it does not do a good job of describing you or who you would like to be, try creating an acronym.

   *Here are some examples:

Grace	Linda	Amarachi
God's	*L*ove	**A**ligned
Rescue	*I*ntuition	**M**arked by God
At	*N*urture	**A**bundant
Crucial	*D*iscernment	**R**ooted in God
Events	*A*lignment	**A**dored, Adorned and Armored by God
		Covered by God
		Highly Favored
		Immersed in God's love

Challenge #1: Who are you? I challenge you to declare who you are each morning, at least 5x a day. This will now be your daily affirmation. Repeat stating who you are until you truly believe it and even afterwards.

Fill in the blank:

I am [insert name].

My name means [insert meaning of name or each acronym].

I believe my life reflects [insert meaning of name and what your name means to you or restate stating each acronym].

I believe that my life is filled with [insert meaning of name and what your name means to you or restate stating each acronym].

And therefore, I am [insert meaning or restate acronyms].

Notes

Chapter 2:

"Why does your hair look like that?"

Growing up, I remember sitting on the living room floor while my mother tightly gripped my hair and wrapped thread around it, which is a common African hairstyle known as *threading*. I remember how me and my sister's hair would stick up in the air sometimes and I never used to mind that hairstyle until elementary school. One day after several stares, one of my friends approached me and asked, *"why does your hair look like that?*" I can even remember someone telling my sister "your hair looks like spider legs." The ridicule we both received for wearing that hairstyle was beyond humiliating and I honestly don't think our mom gave us that hairstyle since.

Instead we got perms, used hot combs, straighteners, and we manipulated our hair so much just to fit in with everyone else and make our hair more "manageable" for us. Oddly enough, that same African hairstyle that we were both so embarrassed to wear was actually a hairstyle meant to protect and grow our hair so that it could flourish. Instead, we were using all of these different harmful chemicals and heat on our hair just to be accepted in society, while simultaneously watching the health of our hair deteriorate. We also neglected to understand our natural hair and its needs and that neglect eventually showed.

I was so used to manipulating my hair, that I didn't realize how my mind was also being manipulated into believing that I actually needed to make these changes to my hair. I believed that having my hair a certain way was the only way to be beautiful or look presentable. And of course, those beliefs were reinforced through the American standard of beauty, schools having restrictions on how to wear your hair, and even the people portrayed in the media. Growing up, there weren't many people on the tv screen or magazine covers that wore and embraced their natural hair or type 4 hair textures. All of the famous women that I looked up to had straight, wavy, loose, or type 3 curly hair.

To this day, I still remember having these two baby dolls when I was between 5 and 7 years old. One was African American with kinky, textured hair, while the other was White with silky straight hair. I remember viewing my Black doll as the "bad doll" because I was taught not to like textured hair and believed that kinky hair meant you looked unkempt and "raggedy." Then I would call my White doll the "good doll" because of its silky hair which was so easy for me to brush through with my toy comb.

It's crazy how I still remember this and how small moments like this shaped how I perceived myself. To a degree, I was learning self-hate. I aspired to have smooth, silky flowing hair like the black girls on the *Just For Me* perm boxes. I remember looking forward to "perm day" growing up and being ready to smooth out all of my kinky new growth. And even though my scalp would burn, I believed that beauty was pain and that taking extreme measures were required to be and remain beautiful.

When I look back, doing things to change the look or the texture of my hair only hurt the health of my hair and I was forced to come to this gut-wrenching realization when I entered college. By my sophomore year of college, I noticed that my hair stopped growing and my ends were breaking off BAD! I couldn't understand why. I had been doing the same things to my hair for the past several years and couldn't figure out why my hair decided to respond differently now. It wasn't until I had several conversations with my more educated, natural hair friends and watched tons of natural hair videos on YouTube, that I understood that the perms I loved so much, didn't necessarily love me back. The perms were not only damaging my hair strands, but also my scalp, and to my surprise, my self-esteem.

Before going natural, I thought I had pretty great self-esteem and self-love, but I quickly learned that the opposite was true. My friends would constantly encourage me to "go natural" and I refused because deep down, I believed that it meant I would be stripping my beauty and self-worth away. I felt that I would no longer be valued, respected, or accepted in the world. And even though I did not believe these things of my friends who were already "natural", I just felt that going natural wouldn't look "good" on me or be good for me. Can you imagine that? I honestly believed that my own natural, God-given hair wouldn't look good on me.

I was raised believing that my hair was my glory, which I still believe it is. However, I thought it meant that my hair needed to look a particular way for me to be proud of it. If I am being completely transparent, I honestly never wanted to go natural, but I was tired of my hair breaking off and I just really wanted my hair to grow. So, I told myself that I would allow my hair to *transition to natural* and I would stop getting perms just until my hair reached my desired length. And in the meantime, I would cover my natural hair with weaves and wigs to hide it. I thought this was a safe and genius master plan!

Well one day, as I was at a college probate, I saw a girl on stage performing her steps with her sorority, and she was rocking her natural hair. But something about this girl and her natural hair was different or maybe it just resonated differently for me that day. After all, I was surrounded by friends who were rocking their beautiful natural hair as well. But something about this girl was majestic and she exuded so much confidence, beauty, and strength that it moved me. Somehow, this girl was able to inspire me and even showed me a glimpse of what I could potentially be if I embraced my natural hair. Her natural hair was her crown and she inspired me to discover my own crown.

So, a few weeks later after the semester had ended, I decided to take out all of the weave and cut off all of my relaxed ends. It felt scary and foolish yet empowering at the same time. And when I finished cutting off all of the relaxed ends and I looked in the mirror, I didn't see the same person. Instead, I saw a more bold, fierce, rooted, and courageous me. Moments later, after I realized what I had done, I quickly felt nervous and vulnerable and wondered how in the world I could go out in public like this. I started thinking of ways I could cover my hair up again to hide my natural hair. I took another long stare in the mirror and then asked myself, how could I fully love myself if I didn't accept and value every God-given part of myself? Why would I allow society to define me when God already told me who I was? So, I challenged myself to remain natural and not wear any weaves for 3 years. I did this to rebuild my sense of worth and love, rediscover my beauty, and feel comfortable in my most natural state.

My journey of going natural forced me to shift my perception from believing my natural hair was "bad" or looked unkempt to understanding that God made no mistakes when He took his time to handcraft me because I am His masterpiece. I needed to understand that I was made in His image and that He made me perfect. And He made you perfect too. You aren't meant to look like everyone else or have anyone else's features. You are meant to look like YOU. Unapologetically you, with every natural kink, coil, curl, and wave and those differences are beautiful. The fact that so many different hair textures exist is beautiful. No texture is superior to the other, they are equally as beautiful and all made in His image, just like you.

Life Lesson 3: You are God's masterpiece.

There is absolutely nothing wrong with deciding not to wear your hair in its natural state because I also love a good weave or press 'n' curl. The real question to ask yourself is why? It's one thing to switch up your hairstyle as a form of art and expression or even as a protective style. But if wearing your natural hair makes you feel like your beauty and value have decreased and faded away, then we have some work to do.

1. What does hair mean for you and how important is the style and look of your hair to you?

2. What do you consider good and bad hair? Which do you consider your hair to be?

3. What are some things you dislike about your natural hair?

4. What are some things you like about your natural hair?

Challenge #2: I challenge you, especially those of you who consider their hair to be "bad" or listed more reasons they disliked their natural hair, to learn more about your hair. This could involve the following:

- Watching YouTube videos to learn more about your specific hair texture and porosity
- Creating a natural hair regimen to safely detangle and properly moisturize your hair
- Discovering the natural hair products your hair responds best to
- Deep conditioning your hair weekly
- Rocking your beautiful natural hair and allowing it to breathe and just be!

Now, look in the mirror and say:

- *I Am Beautiful*
- *I Am God's Masterpiece*
- *My Natural Hair Was Created Perfectly For Me*
- *My Natural Hair Is Perfect For Me*
- *My Natural Hair Is Glorious*
- *My Natural Hair Is Regal*
- *My Natural Hair Beautiful*
- *My Natural Hair Is Enough*

Notes

Chapter 3:

"The country of Africa"

Growing up as an African child in America, I faced a lot of ridicule. It wasn't like now, where African culture is more embraced, celebrated, and seen as cool by the Western world. Back then, and maybe some of you can relate too, some Americans would make fun of African culture and had all of these negative stereotypes and false beliefs. I would get so many ignorant questions and comments about the *"country of Africa"* and what it was like being African, so I took the liberty of listing some below.

- "Can you speak African?"
- "Did you live in a hut?"
- "All Africans smell like fish"
- "African booty scratcher"
- "Africa is so poor"
- "Were you raised with lions and giraffes?"
- "Everyone has AIDS in Africa"
- "Africans are wild and uncivilized"
- "Africa is a country"
- "Africans are violent"

But the comment that I would get from time to time that actually confused me more than annoy me like the other comments was, "you don't look African." Umm…Excuse me? What in the world does that even mean? Like, what does it mean to look African? Was this supposed to be a compliment or an insult? What do all Africans look like to you? There's this big assumption that all Africans have distinct "African features" and these features include being of a darker skin tone, having wide noses, thick lips, brown eyes, and having thick, kinky hair. And yes, some Africans do have these beautiful features, but Africa is a huge CONTINENT filled with several different countries, cultures, and African people. Africans come in all different shades and sizes. Some are lighter skin tones, have more narrow noses, thinner lips, blue eyes, straight, wavy hair. Others have a medium skin tones, brown eyes, curly hair, while others are combination of these different features. No one is more or less African because of their features. Africa is the mother and root where all cultures and races around the world were born. So if we all come from the same place, why is there so much division and separation?

This idea that one race, culture, and features are superior or inferior to the other dates back to slavery. But throughout my experiences, I realized that when someone tries to make you seem inferior or below them because of what you look like, what you have, or who you are, it's honestly a form of self-hate. Think about it, how could someone who is so secure in who they are and truly loves and esteems their self, try to make someone else feel less than?

When you truly feel secure and comfortable in who you are, your actions reflect that. If you truly love yourself, you reflect love onto others. And if you actually dislike or hate yourself or your circumstances, whether you know it or not, you project that hate onto other people. If you feel powerful in your ability and identity, you empower others and build them up. When you feel small on the inside, you make others feel small and say and do things to tear them down. So you see, when people tease and mock you, it really has more to do with them and how they feel about their selves, than it does with you. However, it can also be a form of control. Sometimes when someone feels like they don't have control over something in one area of their lives, they try to force control in another area.

The clearest example of this is demonstrated with bullies. Bullies tend to target people who they perceive as "smaller" or "below" them, whether in size, rank, or role. This is because in their own personal lives, they feel just as small or even smaller. So, in a backwards way, bullies tend to target someone who reminds them of their self. Something about their target reminds them of an area that they are lacking in and by figuratively "stepping on others", they temporarily feel bigger and more accepted. When you're able to take a step back and look at the full picture, you understand that nothing that is done against you really has anything to do with you, but more so to do with that other person.

Life Lesson #4: When people tease and mock you, it really has more to do with them and how they feel about their selves, than it does with you.

Not too long ago, I lived with this roommate who I liked to call "sour face" in my head because every time she saw or spoke to me, it was as if she ate something sour. She literally would complain and pick problems with me every chance she got for no reason at all. As soon as I walked in the room, she had a problem. Even our other roommate (who was close friends with her) told me how she was confused and didn't understand why "sour face" was always trying to create problems with me.

One day, my school hosted this small discussion panel for students planning to go to graduate school and "sour face" was one of the members of the panel. During the discussion, a friend of mine shared with me how she noticed that whenever someone would ask questions concerning the doctoral program and not the master's degree program, "sour face" would turn visibly uncomfortable and bothered. It took this and some other instances of "sour face" sharing her desire for a doctoral degree, for me to realize that it wasn't me personally that she had an issue with, it was the idea of me. Here I was, a Black doctoral student who was always busy with school during the week, while she was a White master's level student who spent majority of her spare time playing with puzzles in the living room.

Now, I am by no means putting down master's degrees, because I even have a master's degree and I worked hard for it! But what I'm saying is, "sour face" clearly wanted to be a doctoral student and probably felt she was more deserving of it than me. And I'm sure seeing me every day just reminded her that she didn't have it and that bothered her. In the words of the famous actor, Denzel Washington, "some people will never like you because your spirit irritates their demons."

Let me take things a step further. Think about how you feel when you receive some really great news or when you get all dressed up and like what you see in the mirror. How do you feel? More than likely, you're feeling really good and your energy and vibrations are high. You are literally feeling like your highest self in that moment. And when you're feeling good, how do you interact with other people? Chances are you're more upbeat, warm and open, and you're even smiling more. And guess what? That energy and vibration is transferring onto other people.

Have you ever noticed when two people are having a conversation, they are often mirroring each other's body language? That is the transfer of energy. When you're having a conversation with someone who appears cold and closed off, all of a sudden you start feel more tense, tight, and closed. And when you talk to someone who is warm, open, and energetic, you start to feel more relaxed, open, energetic, and even uplifted.

So you see, transferring energy can be a good thing and a bad thing. Unfortunately, we can't always control the energy that is being brought upon us, especially if the negative energy is coming from a family member or maybe someone in a position of power. But what we can control is our own energy and our ability to open and close ourselves off to that incoming energy. We literally have the ability to protect our peace and guard our hearts and this is simply by moving out of love.

Life Lesson #5: We can control our own energy and our ability to open and close ourselves off to incoming energy.

When you operate out of love you have more understanding of who you are, what you bring to the table, and you're able to stand firm in that. You also understand that people's feelings about you is really a reflection of how they feel about their self. Operating out of love helps you understand that the real issue isn't with you and truly understanding that is powerful. Love equips you with the power to respond to negative energy with more love. Now, that's definitely much easier said than done. Do you know how hard it is to remain loving when someone wrongs you? It's so difficult and the desire to just go off or respond back with more negativity is so tempting and even feels good in that moment. But in the long term, it only does more harm than good.

Now, I'm not saying be passive and let people walk all over you. You can still be firm and direct and let others know when they are wronging you, but the difference is your delivery. Responding with love allows you to deliver a message from a place of wisdom, understanding, and compassion instead of a place of transferred rage and aggression. Because energy flows freely, it's so easy to receive and release it, but in order to operate out of love, you have to practice and put in effort. Responding with love is a muscle that you have to exercise every day to see progress.

Now, your next question probably is, what is love? Well, that is a whole other book in and of itself. But in short, 1 Corinthians chapter 13 verses 4 through 7 of the *Bible* defines it as this:

"Love is patient, love is kind. It does not envy, it does not boast, it is not proud. It does not dishonor others, it is not self-seeking, it is not easily angered, it keeps no record of wrongs. Love does not delight in evil but rejoices with the truth. It always protects, always trusts, always hopes, always perseveres."

For this section, I want you to take some time and meditate on the scripture, 1 Corinthians 13: 4-7, defining love.

"Love is patient, love is kind. It does not envy, it does not boast, it is not proud. It does not dishonor others, it is not self-seeking, it is not easily angered, it keeps no record of wrongs. Love does not delight in evil but rejoices with the truth. It always protects, always trusts, always hopes, always perseveres."

Try personalizing it and replacing the word "*love*" with "*I*"

I am patient,

I am kind.

I do not envy,

I do not boast,

I am not proud.

I do not dishonor others,

I am not self-seeking,

I am not easily angered,

I keep no record of wrongs.

I do not delight in evil but rejoice with the truth.

I always protect,

I always trust,

I always hope,

I always persevere.

1. What are some ways you can show love to the people in your life?

2. What are some ways you can respond with love when someone is rude or disrespectful towards you?

Challenge #3: I challenge you to respond with love, the next time someone is disrespectful, rude, or tries to make you feel small.

Notes

Chapter 4:

"You're not really African"

When I was a sophomore in college, I worked part-time at my local Macy's department store. I remember, one day, working on the cashier in the children's department and ringing up this woman's items. After she gave me her Macy's card to swipe on the machine, her name popped on the screen and I recognized it and thought, "she must be Nigerian." So, I asked her whether she was, her eyes lit up, and she said yes. She then began to ask me where I was from and when she realized I was not born in Nigeria, her smile quickly turned into a frown and she said, *"you're not really African."*

Can you believe that! So, because I was not born there, I can't call myself African? If both my parents are African and were born there, then what does that make me? I can recall more than a handful of times this type of exchange took place, where someone would tell me I wasn't African because I was born in America. So because I was born in America, I should deny my roots? That's like saying a White person born in Africa is no longer White even though you can visibly see that they are. As far as I'm concerned, my parents are fully African and they raised me as such. The funny thing is, if I had said I was American, and only my parents were African, then I would be told that I'm African too and I should remember where I come from. It's like, no matter what I could have said or where I claimed to be from, I couldn't win with them. To them, I could only be "too American" or "not African enough." Now, isn't that something?

I was always made to feel like I was "not African enough" because I wasn't born there and couldn't speak the language fluently. They assumed that I didn't know anything about my culture and traditions and that I lacked values, morals, and respect. This idea of not being African enough really stuck with me for a while and made me start to question whether I was enough in other areas of my life. I used to contemplate whether I was a good enough daughter or sister, a good enough student, a good enough friend, whether I was smart enough, pretty enough, and whether I was just enough. But then one day I thought to myself, how can a complete stranger tell me who I am? They don't even know me! They don't know my family, my upbringing, the values instilled in me, or my heart. The only thing they do know is where I was born.

This idea and feeling of not being enough didn't just start when I was a sophomore in college. It actually started when I was a child and just stuck with me into adulthood. It was something that just grew and grew over the years and I actually believed it to be true, regardless of any valid proof in my life that proved otherwise. Many of the false ideas and beliefs about ourselves are rooted within us during childhood and follows us into adulthood. It's a phenomenon, a former supervisor of mine introduced to me, known as the child brain versus the adult brain. Many times an idea is planted in us at a young and impressionable age and regardless of how irrational the idea is, we believe it because we are young and naïve, soaking in everything that we hear. We aren't at the stage in development where we have the ability to think more critically about ideas and effectively challenge them.

It's almost like how children believe in Santa Claus. Regardless of how unrealistic it is for an old man to fly in the sky on his reindeer-driven sleigh, squeeze himself through chimneys, and deliver presents to all the kids around the world in just one night, children still believe it. Now, try telling an adult to believe in Santa Claus. They will ask you to prove it with hard concrete evidence and probably tell you one hundred and one reasons why Santa Claus isn't real.

This feeling of not being enough dated back to my pre-teen years. I remember travelling to Nigeria when I was 12 years old and hating every second of being there. During my long four weeks there, I was constantly teased by family members about my

"American accent" and told "I was too American." The family I was so excited to see and bond with were mocking me. Now, what made this really impact me was the fact that my twin sister and younger brother, who were also born and raised in America just like me, weren't being told this, well according to the 12-year-old me's memory. In fact, they were fully embraced and our family liked spending time with them more than with me because they were more relatable. During that trip, I felt so alone and invisible and even came to a point where I began to actually push my family away and isolate myself because I felt like if they weren't going to accept me anyway, why even bother? And guess what? This pattern of pushing family away followed me for a while.

Now looking back at this trip as a self-aware and healed adult, I realized that my family members actually weren't pushing me away. Instead, making fun of me was their way of trying to connect with me.

But because the 12-year-old me was not used to being made fun of like that and was more sensitive and craved acceptance, I was not able to see the bigger picture and my family's efforts to bring me closer actually pushed me away.

Because many of the beliefs and ideas about ourselves are planted within our young child brains, it is important that as we grow older, we are able to reflect and evaluate these same beliefs and ideas with our more developed brains. Once we do, we realize how irrational and even ridiculous most of these ideas and beliefs were in the first place. So, whether I'm "too American" or "not African enough", the truth is I can't please everyone because, frankly, most people don't even know what they want. Some people aren't even pleased with themselves, so how could they possibly be pleased with me?

If you want to be pleased with yourself, you can't rely on other people's opinions of you or let it shape or define you. What really matters is how you feel and what you believe about yourself and standing firm in that. I define who I am. And the truth is, I'm neither "too American" or "not African enough." I'm African and I'm American. I'm African American. I'm the best of both worlds. I'm the best of both cultures. I am the perfect balance. I am me.

Life Lesson #6: If you want to be pleased with yourself, you can't rely on other people's opinions of you or let it shape or define you.

1. What are some beliefs and ideas about yourself that you need to release?

2. When did this belief start?

3. On a scale of 1-10 (1=not true at all, 10=completely true), how much do you actually believe it to be true?

Challenge #4: I challenge you to re-evaluate these

beliefs. List as many reasons as you can why these

beliefs are not true.

Notes

Chapter 5:

"You're not a baby anymore"

During my senior year in high school, I was sitting in the living room with my parents, trying to decide what I should major in college. For some reason I blurted out "how about psychology?" I don't even know why *psychology* popped into my head at the time and to be honest, up until that moment, I actually didn't even know what *psychology* was. And I can absolutely guarantee you that I knew nothing about depression, anxiety, or mental health in general or how complex it was. The only mental health issues I knew about were the ones depicted in African movies when a person would "go mad." I remember how both of my parents' demeanors changed when I popped that question and my father turning down that idea and telling me how I would "go crazy" working with "crazy people."

I think that every person of African descent can relate when I say that mental health is not properly understood and isn't even a priority among many African cultures. Mental health issues like "going mad" are considered taboo or attributed to some curse by an enemy or punishment from God. Even showing too much emotion or struggling to manage emotions all together are looked down upon and considered a sign of weakness. I can remember watching countless African movies where someone had experienced a loss or crisis and had difficulty managing their emotions. And 99.9%

of the time, someone always hit them with the *"you're not a baby anymore"* type of response.

It's like only babies and young children are allowed to show or struggle to manage their emotions and once you reach a certain age, you should magically know how to keep your emotions in check. Talking about emotions and managing them in a healthy way is rare in African culture. When someone is using unhealthy ways to deal with their feelings, the response is always "it's not our culture" or "it's not our way." But what exactly is "our way" and is it really any better?

I remember sitting in the kitchen with my mom when I was in high school and begging her to allow me to transfer schools because I was so unhappy. I went from attending a predominately Black and Hispanic, private Christian school from pre-K to 8th grade, to now attending a predominately White, Catholic high school.

So you can imagine, I went from being around people that looked like me to now being the odd one out. I went from being around people who I shared similar experiences and perspectives with to being around people who I didn't. I went from being *Amarachi* to being "the black girl." I went from being smart and getting good grades to being smart and getting good grades *for a black girl*. And despite my desperate plea to change schools, my mom told me to "just keep going."

Just keep going? Now how was I supposed to do that? Can you expand on this please! One thing I've noticed about African culture is the tendency to embrace pushing feelings aside and "just keep going." On one hand, it demonstrates how resilient we are as a people and how we are able to bounce back. But on another hand, it shows how we avoid and that intention and will for us to be strong, really only makes us weak. Fortunately for me, I was able to work through my struggles and express my emotions in high school through journaling, writing songs, listening to music, and being involved with different activities outside of school. But unfortunately, not everyone is able to do that or even are aware of healthy ways to deal with their struggles.

Most often than not, we aren't given the tools that help us to "just keep going", neither are we taught when it's time to stop the "keep going" plan and exit a situation. Yes, it's great to learn ways to endure the storm and it even helps us to become stronger, but there are circumstances where the best and strongest thing you could ever do is walk away. The plainest example is demonstrated within our culture's pressure for women to get married. Parents are so desperate to quickly marry off their daughters, that teaching them how to recognize red flags and taking time to fully know a potential spouse is not highlighted. Instead, making sure the potential spouse is "successful" and financially stable is put at the forefront. And once married, daughters start to really see who they married and for a few, their once gentle and loving husband has now turned them into a punching bag.

Now, some daughters may run back to their parents for help and some parents will even try to rescue their daughter from the now toxic marriage. However, there are some parents who will encourage their daughter to "just keep going" and endure through the marriage because they don't want them to divorce and return home. Some parents will even question their daughter about what they are doing to make the husband abuse them. Look, I don't care how much you might have pushed or egged someone on, you are not responsible for someone else's actions or decisions. Yes, it's possible to influence it to an extent, but their choice to harm you is completely that, *their choice*. There are also some daughters who, because the "just keep going" mentality is so engraved in them, will decide to stay in the marriage and just struggle in silence.

Life Lesson #7: You are not responsible for someone else's actions or decisions.

Now, let me make myself clear. I am by no means saying that African men or men in general are abusive. That choice falls on the individual. I'm also not encouraging divorce, but would you rather get divorced, have your health, and be single or would you rather stay married and possibly end up in the grave? This may sound extreme, but unfortunately, these things happen! There have been so many cases of women staying in abusive marriages and losing their lives for the sake of keeping their marriages together. I believe that if he's able to raise his hand against you once, he's definitely able to do it again. Is this "just keep going" mindset really worth losing your life? I truly believe that many toxic situations like these could be avoided if we are provided the tools to be able to endure hard situations, as well as taught how to recognize red flags and times when it's best to avoid entering or leaving a toxic situation.

Another layer of this "just keep going" mentality is the idea of not dwelling on a situation or problem in order to move forward. To an extent that is true especially when you're taking it a face value, but you also need to be able think about it on a deeper level so that you can learn from it. I believe everything happens for a reason and most times those reasons are much bigger than us. It's really for you to help other people in similar situations. I believe some of the biggest life lessons we can ever learn are during our darkest hours. So, how can we possibly learn from something we push to the side or sweep under the rug?

Life Lesson #8: Some of the biggest life lessons we can ever learn are during our darkest hours.

The issue with avoidance and not taking the time to work through feelings and hard situations is that it becomes a cycle and you continue to avoid working through other hard situations. All the while, those feelings continue to build up and you begin to actually attract similar difficult situations into your life. Have you ever wondered why you or someone else always find themselves in similar messy or difficult situations? Well, this is exactly why, because those unresolved situations and feelings you are trying your best to bury and hide, are actually being attracted to you. Because you haven't worked through those situations, you also weren't given the opportunity to fully learn from them or learn how to properly move forward and close the door in certain areas of your life.

It's kind of like placing a band aid over a wound that actually needs stitching. Yes, it may be able to mask the wound for a while, but the wound will not be able to properly heal and at some point, will get infected and spread to other areas of your body. I believe God will continue to send you the same tests until you are able to pass it. And sorry to burst many people's bubbles, but avoiding taking the test will not help you pass. You know what happens when you aren't able to pass tests? You eventually fail the class and it impacts your ability to progress. That's the exact same thing in life. As you continue to avoid, you aren't able to learn or apply lessons that would allow you to progress. Instead, you collect more and more unresolved issues and emotions, and at some point, you run out of space to hold those feelings and you pour out. And now, those issues no longer impact just you, but now people around you and possibly even future generations.

I think that as a culture, we have to understand this: we are all human and the most human thing you can ever do in life is feel and have emotions. Regardless of what we are raised to believe, it's 100% okay to feel. It's okay to have emotions. It's okay to feel more than one thing at the same time. It's okay to feel hurt, disappointed, angry, overwhelmed, vulnerable, and so on. There is no right or wrong emotions. It's okay and actually commendable and strong of you to seek therapy. Everyone struggles at times and this does not make you any stronger or weaker of a person. What makes you stronger is what you decide to do with those feelings. And the truth is, the only way you can defeat your giants is by facing them. So do you want to continue to avoid your problems or work through them head on?

Life Lesson #9: The most human thing you can ever do is feel and have emotions.

1. What were you raised to believe about emotions and dealing with problems?

2. What are some problems or situations you feel like you always find yourself in?

3. Why do you think you find yourself in those situations? What do you think those situations says about you?

Challenge #5: I challenge you to reflect! Yes, reflect! Self-reflection is powerful tool that brings forth insight and awareness. Think of some situations you have found yourself in. What were they, were there other people involved, what were their roles, what was your role, what did you do, and how did the situation end? Notice any patterns with the situations, you, and your reactions.

Notes

Chapter 6:

"You must be either a nurse, medical doctor, lawyer, or engineer"

When I was a high school senior starting my college application process, the first thing I thought to myself was "FREEDOM." My 18th birthday was just around the corner and I was finally going to be an adult. I thought this would be my chance to make my very first adult decision without the input of my parents. Well boy was I wrong! I hadn't put much thought into future career options and I actually wasn't sure what I wanted to major in. But I was so excited and ready to explore my vast options because anything would be better than high school.

I started imagining my life as a future actress, fashion designer, teacher, businesswoman, and whatever else sparked my interest at the time. Little did I know, my daydreams would soon be interrupted and put to a complete stop. I soon realized that my options for careers weren't endless, but actually extremely limited. And like what most African kids hear as their parents discuss future careers with them, *"you must be either a nurse, medical doctor, lawyer, or engineer."*

Like you read in chapter 5, my parents quickly shut down my suggestion for majoring in psychology. Instead, my mom told me I needed to study nursing because it was the most stable career option. Don't get me wrong, nursing is a very fulfilling and respectable career. However, I personally have no business being anyone's nurse. The sight of blood makes me weak, the idea of dealing with bodily fluids makes me want to puke, and I found science classes to be quite boring and confusing, despite my ability to pass the classes.

Now I know most parents mean well when they choose our careers for us because they want to ensure that we are secure and stable in life, but we were not placed on this Earth to carry out our parents' dreams. Okay yes, our parents technically were the vessels that brought us into the world, but they didn't choose us like the fruit you buy at a grocery store. They had no control over exactly what we would look like or how our personalities would be or what our real interests, natural gifts, and talents would be. And as much as they may try, they actually don't have full control over our destinies. We do.

God gave each and every one of us this powerful gift called *free will*. He also placed a unique, beautiful, and fulfilling purpose for each of us to pursue if we choose to do so. A lot of people don't realize this, but we actually have the ultimate say in how our life plays out. We can decide if we want to go right or left, front or back, and high or low. Regardless of which door we decide to knock on, each one holds a completely different life and story.

Sometimes our parents' dreams for us to be a nurse, medical doctor, lawyer, or engineer actually do align with our own purpose and dreams and it makes life so much easier especially knowing you have your parents support and approval. But for many people, their parents' dreams and their own actual dreams don't align and it can feel really daunting and confusing. On one hand, you have the option to pursue a road where you are passionate and love what you do, while on the other hand you have the option to pursue a road that your parents are passionate about. You're then faced with deciding whether you will obey your parents' wishes and live up to their expectations of you or step past your parents' wishes and create your own expectations for your life.

Deciding which road to take in life can be a huge and scary decision, especially when you feel like going against your parents' dreams means that you are disobeying them. The thing about our parents' dreams for us is that it's safe, but it's also limiting. Not only is it a limitation on our options and chances for exploring in life, but it is also a limitation on our potential and abilities. In some cases, it can prevent people from even having the opportunity to discover their gifts, talents, and favorite hobbies especially when they started living out their parents' dreams at a young age. The truth is, people place limitations on your potential and dreams because deep down, that is the limitation that they believe about their selves.

Life Lesson #10: People place limitations on your potential and dreams because deep down, that is the limitation that they believe about their selves.

Although most parents usually know what's best for their kids, placing limitations on their child's dreams and future actually does more harm than good. In reality, it places limits in how much we can learn, grow, earn, and LIVE! Benjamin Franklin once said, "most people die at 25 and aren't buried until they're 75." The first time I heard this quote, my mind was blown. The idea that so many people physically live until the age of 75, but die internally at 25 is sad. When you choose to live out someone else's dreams, you essentially kill your own. Yes, having a job that pays well and has benefits is the safe thing to do, but it is not the only job that can earn you money. In 2021, you can make money doing almost ANYTHING. When you're working a job that you're not passionate about, at some point the money will not be enough to keep you motivated or interested. Living a life where you're doing things that you aren't passionate about or find fulfilling can feel draining and robotic. And at some point, you will feel completely empty and like you are no longer living.

As fate would have it, my parents' plan for me to be a nursing major hit a roadblock in the beginning. Luckily for me (although it didn't feel like luck at the time) my SAT scores prevented me from being accepted into the nursing program at my school of choice, so I opted to start my major as *undecided*. The plan was that I would take some prerequisite courses towards the nursing program and prove myself to be a strong candidate when I eventually applied. And that's exactly what I did. I followed the plan and made sure that I earned good grades and a good gpa that would secure me a place in the nursing program.

Then on April 1st, 2014, my life changed forever. The day I had been working towards was here and I had finally received my decision email. To my surprise and dismay, it was a rejection email. Up until that moment, the plan was going so smoothly that I didn't even think twice at the idea that I might get rejected. I also didn't consider whether the plan was something I actually really wanted to follow through on or not, I just knew I was expected to. My world was completely turned upside down and my heart was broken. I had been working tirelessly to reach my parents' goals and was beyond hurt that all my efforts did not pay off. I felt like a complete failure and a disappointment. Despite my rejection, I had to fulfill my parents' goals and expectations by any means necessary, so I decided to reapply to an accelerated nursing program the following year.

As crazy as it sounds, it turns out that my rejection was the best thing that ever happened to me. It gave me the unique opportunity to reevaluate whether nursing was a career I truly wanted or whether there was something else I was called to do. I had a chance to figure out what my interests, strengths, and natural abilities were and what would make me feel most fulfilled. I had a chance to get to know the real me and look beyond my role as a daughter.

One year later, I received my decision email and this time it was a letter of acceptance into the nursing program yet, I was not excited. All my hard work had finally paid off, but I didn't feel accomplished. I had finally figured out who I was and the closer my start date within the program approached, the more reluctant and heavier my heart felt. I felt so much pressure to fulfill my parents' expectations of me, yet sick to my stomach that I might potentially throw away my chances of living a purpose filled life.

Every day I desperately prayed to God for a miracle. I kept asking Him to save me from having to go down a road that wasn't meant for me. The funny thing is, as I was praying to God for a breakthrough, He was preparing me to BREAK THROUGH! As the days passed, I became more and more uncomfortable in my situation and more and more ready for a change, even if it meant that I physically had to do something to cause the change. Sometimes we pray for God to change our situation and save us, not realizing that He places the courage and strength within us so that we can save ourselves by His strength and spirit. Sometimes that situation that makes us feel powerless, God will use to make us become powerful. And that situation that was meant to make us a victim, He will use to make us a victor.

So, after a lot of prayer and fasting, I decided to make a bold and crazy move. A move that changed my life forever. I dropped out of the nursing program. And there I was. Many would say I was young and dumb. I had no real solid plan, but I definitely had crazy faith because I knew God would guide me. I knew His plans for me were good and worth taking that huge leap of faith, so I did. I had so much faith in God that even when some friends and a pastor told me I made the wrong decision, I did not budge. Instead, I stood strong and firm in my faith because I knew there was so much more to my life than fulfilling someone else's dreams. But no one said that road would be easy.

Although, my father was supportive because he saw how unhappy I was, my mother was beyond upset and disappointed. One of the most painful feelings to ever bear is your parents' disappointment. That summer living back home was not easy. Although we lived in a moderately spacious home, I felt the walls caving in on me. It came to a point that every single morning, like clockwork, my mom would call me into her bedroom and drill me about what I was doing with my life. I honestly had no idea, but I was trusting and believing in God to lead me.

Now, I am by no means telling you to quit your jobs or drop out of school. Don't put that on me! It is certainly possible for you to fulfill someone else's dreams and pursue your own dreams at the same time, especially when someone else's dreams financially allow you to pursue your own. But I will pose this question: Is living out someone else's dreams worth killing yours?

Believe it or not, that "random" idea that popped in my head back in high school, was actually the route God told me to pursue. Throughout college, I had actually taken several psychology courses and was so intrigued and excited about this whole new world. For the first time in my life, I was educated on the brain and behavior and I had the potential to bring awareness and normalize mental health among people of color. I was able to understand people on a much deeper level and stand as an example for other people around me who were afraid to take a leap of faith. The thing about purpose is that it's not just about you. Your purpose serves and impacts other people. Everything we do has a consequence. And whether you decide to pursue or not pursue your purpose impacts not just you, but people around you. If we actually knew all the lives that are impacted by our life decisions, I'm sure we'd all strive to make better choices.

Les Brown once said that "the graveyard is the richest place on earth" because it is filled with so many unfulfilled dreams, hopes, inventions, cures, songs, and books that people were afraid to follow through. Now, you have a powerful and life changing choice to make. You can decide whether you want to live out your parents' dreams or live on purpose. Each path consists of a different story. Which path will you decide to take?

Life Lesson #11: You are much more than your parents'
expectations of you.

1. What are you passionate about?

2. What do you believe you have been called to do in your life?

3. How does this calling serve and help other people?

Challenge #6: I challenge you think about your life.

Now, I am not asking you to make any decisions, but I want you think about your life story and how your life would look if you pursued other peoples' dreams for you versus if you pursued your own dreams and purpose.

Notes

_____

_____

_____

_____

_____

_____

_____

_____

_____

_____

_____

_____

_____

_____

Chapter 7:

"See your mates"

Taking that leap of faith to pursue your purpose is not always a smooth and easy road to travel. To be quite frank, it could be one of the scariest and possibly even the hardest thing you ever do in your life. And for a lot of people, just the idea of taking that leap intimidates them back into playing it safe and sticking to the same old things. I remember back when I was in the process of planning to drop out of my nursing program and unsure of what would happen next. I just assumed that because I was choosing to live on purpose, my life would get easier and opportunities would flow freely to me because I removed all of the things blocking me from pursuing my purpose. I honestly thought that because I showed up for my purpose, opportunities would instantly land on my lap. I am here to tell you today that I was 100% wrong! If you're thinking that following your dreams/purpose means living an easier life filled with sunshine, roses, rainbows, and butterflies, then girl... WAKE UP!

Living on purpose is not that simple and to be real with you, if it was that easy then everyone would do it! Pursuing purpose can be a narrow, lonely, and even challenging path and there might even be moments where you feel like giving up because things aren't lining up when you expect them to and you find yourself constantly facing obstacles and being moved out of your comfort zone. What makes things even harder is that as soon as your disapproving African parents see that your life choices aren't immediately taking off and prospering, they lecture you and, at some point, compare you to your peers with their famous line, *"See Your Mates!"*

Man, do African parents love comparing you to other people's kids whom they honestly know nothing about! They have no clue what those people did to even get where they are (good, bad, ugly, and so on) or how they even feel about the things they have accomplished. It's almost like their sole focus is on the accomplishment itself and not on the journey you take to achieve it. I'm sure we all know how African parents love to introduce their children by their accomplishments like "this is my son, the medical doctor" or "this is my daughter, the lawyer." And when African parents have no accomplishment to introduce or flaunt you by to friends and families, it's a big problem and they start to compare you to aunty "so-and-so's" kid, the medical doctor or the lawyer. They say things like "why can't you be more like them", "your mates are medical doctors, engineers, lawyers, etc.", "Lord, why is my own different", and even "I did not shame my parents so you will not shame me!" The comparison can be so much that it feels like, if you're not doing as good or better than aunty "so-and-so's" kid, then you are failing at life.

Theodore Roosevelt once said "comparison is the thief of joy." When you focus on what everyone else has or are doing, it robs you of the ability to appreciate what you have and the progress you have made. Most times, you might even be doing better than the other person, but your blinded by the few things in their lives you have access to see, that you can't see the full picture. Take me for example. From the outside looking in, I am an educated woman with two degrees, and currently working towards my doctoral degree. So, the average person would assume that I'm doing pretty great for myself. But what people don't see are the number of obstacles and hardships I've faced throughout this journey.

People looking from the outside can't see how I used to walk on eggshells because I was living in and attending a predominately white university, constantly worried about being perceived as a "threat" and having my hard-work and dreams taken away from me. They can't see how I had to censor myself so I wouldn't be labeled as "sassy" or "angry". They can't see how lonely and unsupported it feels to be a Black girl at a predominately white school and area. They can't see the hoops that I've had to jump through or things I've had to learn on my own (outside of academics) because I am the first in my immediate family to even reach this level of academia. They couldn't see the amount of rejection I faced before and even more so, throughout my doctoral studies. And most of all, no one saw the many nights I cried or felt like giving up and dropping out of school. I say all this to say, sometimes the grass isn't greener. Just because it looks like aunty "so-and-so's" kid's life is "together" or "better", doesn't mean it actually is. They could literally be hanging on to a single thread and a dream.

I should note that not everyone's experience of pursuing their purpose is like this. Some purpose walks are smoother, some are rockier, some might be quicker, and some could be longer. Everyone's purpose walk and estimated time of "arrival" is different. Your purpose and journey are just that, YOURS. And there is a time and season for everything. There's a time for learning and preparing for the journey and there is a time for putting those learned skills to action to walk out that journey. There is also a time for facing the results of your actions (or movement) and facing the results of your lack of action.

What I am basically trying to say is that we all go through different seasons in our lives and it's important to be aware of the season and time period you currently are in. It's so easy to feel like you need to rush or get on the same schedule or "level" with someone else, but you actually don't. Just because aunty "so-and-so's" kid is pursuing [blank], doesn't mean you have to pursue the same thing or that your experience and journey will be the same. Everyone's purpose journey or route is different. And we all have and operate on different timelines and schedules. Unfortunately, society makes us feel like we have to "hustle and bustle" and by age [blank], we should be successful and financially independent and free. That is not everyone's story or path in life. Neither is overnight success. So, comparing your journey to someone else's is not only unfair, but a disservice to yourself and a complete waste of time and energy.

Life Lesson #12: Everyone's purpose map/route is different and we all operate on different timelines and schedules.

Someone might be wondering what happens when trying to live on purpose becomes too difficult and you don't get that immediate gratification that society makes us believe we should have? There's this popular lie that many people believe today and it's that when things aren't working out for you, then it's a sign that you should try something else. And sometimes it actually might be the case that you need to be *redirected* to try something else, but that's not always the case. Sadly, many people have twisted and turned the concept of *redirection* into this quitting mentality once life gets a little too hard. This skewed *redirection* idea reinforces society's belief and need for immediate gratification; and now many people assume that when something is too challenging or requires "too much" effort, they should give up.

Thoughts like "this shouldn't be this hard", "nothing has happened yet", and "maybe I would have been better off if I didn't take this leap of faith" can make you second-guess whether or not you're making the right decision. When your purpose plan doesn't pan out as expected, it's easy and normal to feel discouraged, especially when people around you and on social media seem to be living their best life. It's even harder when you scroll down your timeline on social media, and all you see are people posting their accomplishments, celebrations, and traveling the world. Meanwhile, you feel a sense of stagnancy and you're struggling to get by or reach your goals. But this feeling doesn't mean you should give up entirely.

When we look at some of the most successful people in the world, most of them didn't become who they are overnight. It took Beyoncé several years before she got her first big hit with Destiny's child and an additional 6 years before she got her first big hit as a solo artist. I repeat, it took YEARS! What if Beyoncé would have given up her singing career because she wasn't an overnight success or wasn't well received by a crowd, earlier in her career. Can you actually imagine a musical and entertainment world without the impact of Beyoncé? Beyoncé never quit, but instead remained persistent and kept working until she eventually made a powerhouse name for herself. And the same can happen for you. You also have something big inside of you to share with the world. It may not be the exact same as Beyoncé, but it WILL make an impact.

Here's another example. Recently, I applied for my doctoral internship, which is a requirement for graduation and licensure. If anyone knows anything about the national matching system, the whole application process and interviewing is very stressful and expensive. However, I had all my essays prepared, applied to a bunch different sites, and spent several LONG hours participating in interviews. Well, Match day arrived and I found out that I did not match to any site, meaning I was not offered an internship placement. Of

ALL the sites that I applied to and interviewed with, NOT ONE of them selected me. I was shocked! There I was, I had everything that was needed including my experience and training, my application materials, my organization, and my professionalism. I followed the plan, but it didn't work! I didn't even predict that there could be a chance I wouldn't match because I was so confident in my application and interviews. I felt so confused, hurt, discouraged, and a little defeated. And to add salt to injury, I was told that I was the ONLY person in my program who didn't match for internship. I never felt so small, inferior, humiliated, and alone in my life, than I did in that moment.

So what did I do? Truthfully, I took a few days to sulk and feel all of these different emotions I was experiencing because there was no way I could focus on anything else at the time. Now, I could have given up or waited another year to apply again, but I didn't. I could've easily believed that maybe this road wasn't meant for me, especially since I had all of the qualifications necessary and then some. I could've assumed that maybe this rejection meant that I needed to quit and be "redirected" to a completely different field. But I refused to believe that or give up and just kept my eyes on the prize.

I eventually decided to apply for phase 2 of the matching process and hoped for the best. And guess what? I matched! I shared this story because I want you to know that there might be a time when you prepare and even over prepare for something and it still might not go as planned or in your favor. But this doesn't make you incapable or inferior to someone else, neither does it mean you should give up. It just means that you have to try again and possibly take a different approach to it.

When you keep knocking and beating on a wall, eventually it'll tear down.

The thing about living on purpose is that those challenges and roadblocks that you face serve a purpose. They could be protecting you from something that you might not be ready for or even need, but most importantly they are meant to train and mold you to live a more intentional, clear, passionate, and impactful life. So, when one door closes, try going through another door or even a window! The key point here is that you don't give up. Now, you may need to make a "pit stop" or take a break so you can rest, reset, or re-route, but that is okay, as long as you get back on the road and keep trying.

So dear African American girl, you can do whatever you put your mind to. You are your only limit. If you don't lose hope and remain persistent, you WILL reach your goals. You are not too late or moving to slow. There is no competition with anyone else. Don't get caught up and distracted in how much time has passed or your number of successes. God chose YOU to pursue this purpose because YOU, and only YOU, are the BEST person to fulfill it. God believes in you and so do I. African American girl, you got this!

Challenge #7: Now that you've had some time to think about what your purpose might be, I want you to think about your purpose map and what it might look like so far. I want to help you start to think about and plan your goals. Sometimes, it's a straight route, but there are times when we reach an obstacle or dead end and need to take a different route. There are also times when you face multiple obstacles and dead ends and need to figure out multiple new routes. Try writing out different steps you need to take to reach your goals. Also try creating backup plans, when one step doesn't work out. Try this exercise to help you map out plan. Good Luck!

Your Purpose Map

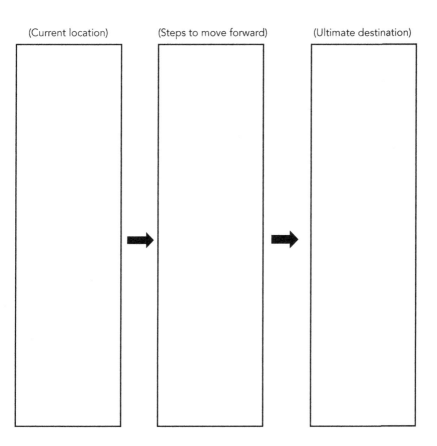

(Current location)

(Steps to move forward)

(Ultimate destination)

Your Purpose Map

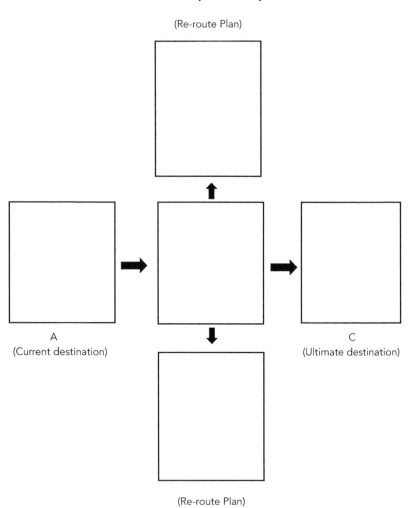

(Re-route Plan)

A
(Current destination)

C
(Ultimate destination)

(Re-route Plan)

Notes

_____

_____

_____

_____

_____

_____

_____

_____

_____

_____

_____

_____

_____

_____

Dear African American Girl,

Being from 2 different worlds and 2 different cultures can at times feel assuring, confusing, lonely, embracing, encouraging, discouraging, exhausting, and empowering all at the same time. Many times, one world could encourage an idea or piece of your identity, while the other shames it and pushes it away.
But what you must remember in both worlds is this:

You were not meant to blend in or be ordinary.
You are God's masterpiece. You're meant to stand out.
Your name is your power. Your hair is your crown.
Your eyes see beyond the present.
Your ears hear deep into the soul.
Your mind and imagination are endless.
Your love heals. Your voice brings life.
Your hands create. Your footprints impact.
Your complexity makes you perfect.
So stand firm in your identity because you are limitless.

With Love,
Amarachi

Connect With Amarachi

Instagram→ *@amarachi_aa*

YouTube→ *Graceologist*

Made in the USA
Middletown, DE
22 December 2022

20080400R00070